"When the whole world is silent, even **one voice** becomes **powerful**."
—Malala Yousafzai

For my own truth-seeking children—Maya, Jaden, and Rahm
—P.B.

To all the courageous children standing up for justice, fighting
for gender and racial equality, and fighting for clean air and water.
I admire you. Your voice matters.
—S.C.

Text copyright © 2021 by Preet Bharara

Jacket and interior illustrations copyright © 2021 by Sue Cornelison

All rights reserved. Published in the United States by Crown Books for Young Readers,
an imprint of Random House Children's Books, a division of Penguin Random House LLC, New York.

Crown and the colophon are registered trademarks of Penguin Random House LLC.

Visit us on the Web! rhcbooks.com
Educators and librarians, for a variety of teaching tools,
visit us at RHTeachersLibrarians.com

Library of Congress Cataloging-in-Publication Data
Names: Bharara, Preet, author. | Cornelison, Sue, illustrator.
Title: Justice is ... / written by Preet Bharara ; illustrated by Sue Cornelison.
Description: First edition. | New York : Crown Books for Young Readers, [2021] |
Audience: Ages 4–8 | Audience: Grades Pre-K–3 | Summary: "Introduce
the concept of justice to young people with this picture book by former
US attorney for the Southern District of New York and *New York Times*
bestselling author of *Doing Justice,* Preet Bharara"— Provided by publisher.
Identifiers: LCCN 2021005438 (print) | LCCN 2021005439 (ebook) | ISBN 978-0-593-17662-7
(hardcover) | ISBN 978-0-593-17666-5 (library binding) | ISBN 978-0-593-17665-8 (ebook)
Subjects: LCSH: Justice—Juvenile literature.
Classification: LCC JC578 .B458 2021 (print) | LCC JC578 (ebook) | DDC
320.01/1—dc23

The text of this book is set in 20-point Chronicle Text Roman.

The illustrations in this book were created using a stylus Wacom Cintiq
in Photoshop with a charcoal pen tool.

MANUFACTURED IN SINGAPORE

10 9 8 7 6 5 4 3 2 1   First Edition

Justice Is...

A Guide for Young Truth Seekers

Written by
PREET BHARARA

Illustrations by
SUE CORNELISON

Crown Books for Young Readers
New York

Justice is important.
It takes hard work . . .
and an open mind.

To find Justice, ask all kinds of people to join your search. Justice needs to hear every side of the story.

Sonia Sotomayor—US Supreme Court Justice

Justice asks questions, lots of them.

Justice isn't afraid
to right a wrong.

JOIN THE
NATIONAL
WOMAN
SUFFRAGE
ASSOCIATION

Standing up for Justice can get lonely.

Elizabeth Eckford—School Integration Activist

It can even be dangerous.
But Justice is worth the risk.

Justice can be slow.

It can even be denied—for a time.

Japanese American Internees

Tenement Slums

Sometimes people worry

Slavery

that there is no Justice in the world.

But don't lose hope.
Justice is always there—
waiting for good people
to find their voices.

Harvey Milk—LGBTQ Activist and Trailblazing Gay Elected Official

Waiting for brave people to stand up together.
Because Justice can't do it alone.
At times it needs an army at its back.

Sometimes one clear voice can shine through the darkness and say, "This is not right!"

But we must always stand watch,
because Injustice is always waiting too.
We the people must make laws to protect Justice.

And we must make sure

that no one is above the law.

Richard Nixon—First US President to Resign

Because Justice matters! Together we can make the world a better place for everyone.

They Stood for Justice

Frederick Douglass, the most famous Black man of his time, was welcomed by President **Abraham Lincoln** when he showed up at the White House uninvited to discuss the unfair treatment of Black soldiers. Lincoln's respect for Douglass led to the men meeting two more times before Lincoln was assassinated.

Sonia Sotomayor became the first person of Puerto Rican descent and the third woman justice when President Barack Obama named her to the Supreme Court in 2009. She has been a champion for the powerless and underrepresented.

Ida B. Wells was an investigative journalist who reported on civil rights matters, risking her own safety to shine a spotlight on lynching and white violence against Black people in the late nineteenth century. She also fought for women's right to vote.

Sojourner Truth escaped from slavery and became a famous abolitionist, orator, and suffragist. Her "Ain't I a Woman?" speech gained powerful support for women's right to vote, even though many white suffragists did not support Black women—or men—being granted that right too.

Elizabeth Eckford was one of the first Black students to integrate an all-white high school in Little Rock, Arkansas, in 1957. The fifteen-year-old was threatened and stopped from entering the school on her first day but persevered and completed her freshman year.

Malala Yousafzai was fifteen when she was shot by the Taliban because she fought for her right, and the right of all girls, to go to school. She survived, continued to speak out, and won a Nobel Peace Prize.

Nelson Mandela was imprisoned for twenty-seven years for his militant fight against apartheid, the forced segregation of all people of color in South Africa. When he was released in 1990, he sought reconciliation instead of violence, negotiated an end to apartheid, and won a Nobel Peace Prize. In 1994, the former prisoner became president of the country he helped heal.

Japanese American Internees were forced into "relocation camps," falsely suspected of collaborating with Japan after it attacked Pearl Harbor. An estimated 120,000 people from the western United States were held captive for most of World War II, with the last camp closing in March 1946.

Harvey Milk was a human rights activist and one of the first openly gay elected officials in America until a former colleague murdered him and San Francisco mayor George Moscone in their city hall offices on November 27, 1978. Harvey's death helped spark a national movement for LGBTQ rights.

Black Lives Matter was founded in 2013 to stop institutional racism and violence against the Black community, then grew to become one of the largest social movements in American history after the killing of George Floyd in May 2020 sparked global outrage.

Mohandas Gandhi led thousands of Indians on a 240-mile march to the sea to protest English control of India. When they reached the shore, he taught them to make their own salt, which was against English law. Gandhi and his followers were arrested, but the Salt March was an important first step toward Indian independence.

John Lewis was a giant of the civil rights movement and a follower of Dr. Martin Luther King Jr.—who taught him to practice nonviolence—even when John was beaten and jailed for protesting. He later became known as the "conscience of the Congress," after being elected and serving for over three decades in the government that had long denied his right to vote.

Richard Nixon became the first and only president of the United States to resign, to avoid being impeached and removed from office for his role in the Watergate scandal. Brave investigative journalists and their newspapers risked their careers to expose his corruption, believing that no American is above the law.

"Truth never damages
a cause that is just."
—Mohandas Gandhi